FLOODED IN FORT LAUDERDALE:

Comprehensively Understanding the Causes, Impacts and Solutions

ANGELA PETERS

TABLE OF CONTENTS

CHAPTER 1

Introduction: Overview and Historical context of the Fort Lauderdale flooding problem

Fort Lauderdale, a coastal city in Florida, has been plagued by floods for decades, and the situation has only become worse in recent years. All parties involved must give the flooding situation in Fort Lauderdale their immediate attention since it is a complicated subject with many causes, effects, and possible remedies.

The flooding issue in Fort Lauderdale is not a recent occurrence, and climate change, increasing sea levels, and urbanization have all made it worse. Due to its low-lying geography and insufficient drainage, the city is especially susceptible to floods. The problem has become worse as a result of the region's growing storm frequency and severity.

Due to its geographic position and natural phenomena like hurricanes, tidal shifts, and excessive rainfall, Fort Lauderdale has historically been plagued by floods. The city is situated in a low-lying region and is bordered by waterways including the New River, Intracoastal Waterway, and the Atlantic Ocean. The city's drainage systems were built to manage stormwater runoff, but owing to fast urbanization, an increase in impervious surfaces, and changes in precipitation patterns, the system is now overloaded.

Hurricanes and storm surges caused considerable flooding in Fort Lauderdale in the **1940s** and **1950s**. The city's drainage systems were further impacted by the **1960s** and **1970s** building surge. The city's drainage systems were overburdened as a result of the increasing building and road development, which decreased the number of permeable surfaces and increased stormwater runoff.

Due to the consequences of climate change, the flooding issue in Fort Lauderdale became worse throughout the **1990s** and **2000s**. The flooding issue has become increasingly severe, frequent, and unexpected due to rising sea levels, an increase in the frequency of extreme weather events, and changes in precipitation patterns. High tides have caused flooding in the city on sunny days as well, a phenomenon known as sunny-day flooding.

YEAR	CASES
1947	Hurricane
1950	Severe Flooding due to heavy rainfall
1960	Hurricane Donna caused extensive flooding and damage to property
1977	Severe flooding due to heavy rainfall, resulting in several deaths and significant property damage
1996	Hurricane Irene caused minor flooding in low-lying areas
2000	Severe flooding due to heavy rainfall

2015	King tides caused coastal flooding in low-lying areas, including downtown Fort Lauderdale and Las Olas Boulevard
2016	Hurricane Matthew caused minor flooding and damage to property in Fort Lauderdale and surrounding areas
2017	Hurricane Irma caused significant flooding and damage to property in Fort Lauderdale and surrounding areas
2021	Tropical Storm Eta caused significant flooding and damage to property in Fort Lauderdale, particularly in low-lying areas

As you observe in the table above, flooding has been a persistent issue in Fort Lauderdale for years, with several large disasters happening as a result of torrential rain and tropical weather systems. Recent years have seen an increase in flooding issues, especially in low-lying regions of the city, as a result of the effect of increasing sea levels brought on by climate change.

Fort Lauderdale has put in place several strategies to deal with the flooding issue in recent years. These actions include elevating roadways in flood-prone regions, building pump stations, and enhancing drainage systems. These steps, however, have not been enough to lessen the effects of floods on the city.

The consequences of climate change, such as increasing sea levels, an increase in the frequency of severe weather events, and changes to precipitation patterns, have made the issue worse. These elements have increased Fort Lauderdale's flooding problem's severity, regularity, and unpredictability.

The flooding issue in Fort Lauderdale has wide-ranging and substantial effects. Damage to property, and infrastructure, and lost tourism-related income are only a few examples of the economic effects. The negative effects on the environment include harm to ecosystems, a decline in biodiversity, and the development of waterborne illnesses. The social effects include the eviction of inhabitants, interference with daily routines, and harm to the public's health and safety.

The effects of floods in Fort Lauderdale have been lessened by several measures. These remedies include anything from long-term infrastructure expenditures to quick emergency fixes. Creating flood response strategies, setting up temporary flood barriers, and enhancing drainage systems are some of the short-term approaches. Implementing green infrastructure like rain gardens, bioswales, and permeable pavements, enhancing flood protection structures like sea walls, and funding environmentally friendly transportation options like bicycling and walking are some long-term alternatives.

Due to the consequences of climate change, Fort Lauderdale's long-standing flooding problem has become worse. Because of the city's geographic position, rising development, and shifting precipitation patterns, the drainage systems are overburdened, which has a substantial effect on the city's economy, ecology, and social well-being. To create comprehensive and potent remedies that might lessen the effects of flooding on the city, it is essential to thoroughly research the historical background of the flooding issue.

It's crucial to extensively research the causes, effects, and possible remedies to solve the flooding issue in Fort Lauderdale. Natural elements like rainfall, tidal fluctuations, and storms as well as human actions like changes in land use, inadequate drainage systems, and inadequate flood protection measures are some of the causes of floods. It is essential to research these variables to create complete and successful flood mitigation strategies.

CHAPTER 2

Causes of Flooding in Fort Lauderdale - Natural and study of the impact of urbanization on the flooding issue

In Fort Lauderdale, a city in Florida, flooding is a recurring issue. In addition to other natural and man-made variables, the city's position on a coastal plain makes flooding accidents more common. This chapter will look at both natural and man-made elements that contribute to flooding in Fort Lauderdale. We'll also examine how urbanization contributes to the flooding issue becoming worse.

Natural Elements That Cause Flooding

Because of its coastal position and closeness to various bodies of water, including the Atlantic Ocean and the Everglades, Fort Lauderdale is susceptible to floods. Tropical storms, hurricanes, and a lot of rain are frequent events that might cause flooding in the city. Moreover, the city's low-lying topography—it rises only 9 feet above sea level—worsens the effects of natural flooding incidents.

hurricanes and tropical storms: Florida's coast, where Fort Lauderdale is situated, is subject to hurricanes and tropical storms. High rains and strong winds brought on by these weather events may result in floods and property damage.

Natural Elements That Cause Flooding are:

- Heavy rains: During the rainy season, Fort Lauderdale suffers strong rains, which may cause flash floods. This issue is made worse by the city's low-lying terrain since rainfall cannot simply drain away from low-lying places.

- High tides: Fort Lauderdale is situated on the Intracoastal Canal, which connects to the ocean via the city's various canals. Seawater may enter the canals at high tides and overflow into low-lying regions, resulting in floods.

- Factors Caused by Human Activity that Lead to Flooding. Flooding in Fort Lauderdale is caused by artificial activity as well as natural causes. The complex system of canals and streams in the city may overflow during times of severe rainfall or high tides, causing flooding in low-lying regions. This system was meant to regulate floods and give recreational possibilities. The ability of the soil to absorb rainfall is further decreased by urban expansion and land-use changes, such as the replacement of natural land cover with impermeable surfaces like concrete and asphalt, which causes increased runoff and floods.

- Urbanization: As Fort Lauderdale has expanded, impermeable surfaces like concrete and asphalt have risen in number. Due to the decreased ability of the ground to absorb precipitation, drainage, and floods are enhanced.
- Changes in land use: The infiltration capacity of the land may be decreased by replacing natural land cover with impermeable surfaces, which can increase runoff and floods.

- Management of the canal system: Fort Lauderdale has a vast system of canals that were constructed for flood control and recreational uses. However poor management of these canals, such as insufficient dredging and upkeep, may cause overflows that cause floods.
- Stormwater infrastructure: Localized flooding results from the city's outdated stormwater infrastructure's inability to manage the amount of water during severe rainstorm events.
- Sea-level rise: As a result of climate change, the sea level is rising, which makes flooding in low-lying locations like Fort Lauderdale more frequent and severe.

Study of the impact of urbanization on the flooding issue

Urban growth has a huge impact on Fort Lauderdale's flooding issue. The number of impermeable surfaces, such as concrete and asphalt, has increased as the city has expanded and developed, which lowers the ability of the ground to absorb rainfall. Increased runoff and floods have resulted from this, especially in low-lying regions.

Also, the reduction in the land's ability to absorb water due to the replacement of natural land cover with impermeable surfaces has increased runoff and floods. The city's drainage patterns have changed as a result of urbanization, which may make flooding issues worse. Insufficient stormwater infrastructure, such as deteriorating pipes and culverts, may also be a factor in urban floods.

In addition to these elements, Fort Lauderdale's flooding issue has also been exacerbated by the construction of canals for flood control and recreational uses. These canals can overflow and flood as a result of improper management, including poor maintenance and dredging.

It's crucial to remember that urbanization is not the only factor contributing to Fort Lauderdale's flooding issue. Natural elements including prolonged periods of heavy rain and high tides also significantly contribute to the city's flooding incidents.

In Fort Lauderdale, there is a need for improved land-use planning and stormwater management techniques to address the contribution of urban growth to the flooding issue. This might include preserving natural land cover, using green infrastructure, and managing and maintaining stormwater infrastructure and canals appropriately. To lessen the number of impervious surfaces in the city, it could also be necessary to reevaluate present development strategies and zoning laws.

In conclusion, although urban expansion has contributed to Fort Lauderdale's flooding issue, it is crucial to take a variety of variables into account while tackling this problem. To lessen the consequences of floods in the city, a thorough strategy that takes into account both human and natural elements is required.

CHAPTER 3

Impacts of Flooding in Fort Lauderdale
Social, economic, and environmental impacts of flooding and effects of flooding on the community

In Fort Lauderdale, flooding could have a big social influence on the neighborhood. The following are a few societal repercussions of floods in Fort Lauderdale:

- Displacement: People's lives may be severely disrupted when flooding forces them to leave their homes and seek safety elsewhere. People may sometimes have to leave their homes for lengthy periods, which may cause worry, tension, and uncertainty.
- Health risks: Both humans and animals may be in danger from ingesting toxic substances found in floodwaters, such as sewage, chemicals, and debris. Skin irritations, respiratory issues, and gastrointestinal ailments may result from

exposure to polluted water. Respiratory problems may also be caused by mold development in moist conditions.

- Psychological stress: For individuals who are impacted, flooding may be a terrible event that leaves them feeling scared, anxious, and powerless. Social isolation, a sense of loss, and concern about the future are common among the displaced.
- Social relationships may be broken by flooding, which can also damage local commerce. Individuals may face a breakdown in trust and social cohesiveness, lose access to neighborhood services and resources, and feel separated from their neighbors.
- Economic hardship: Flooding may have a considerable negative impact on a person's or family's finances, especially if they are already having financial difficulties. The cost of repairing and replacing damaged property may be high, and losing money as a result of company closures or missed work can make matters worse.

The community of Fort Lauderdale may suffer serious economic effects from flooding. In Fort Lauderdale, flooding will have the following financial effects among others:

- Property damage: Flooding may seriously harm buildings, infrastructure, and possessions, necessitating expensive repairs and lost income. Damage to plumbing and electrical systems, as well as damage to personal goods, are all examples of property damage.

- Flooding may cause supply chains to break down, forcing companies to temporarily or permanently shut their doors, and resulting in lost sales and income. Particularly small firms may find it difficult to recover from the financial effects of floods.

- Tourism and recreation: Fort Lauderdale's tourist and recreation sector, a significant source of income for the city, is susceptible to the effects of flooding.

Events that are postponed, canceled, or cause damage to attractions may cost companies and the community money.

- Damage to infrastructure: Flooding may interrupt crucial services and cause serious damage to important infrastructure, including highways, bridges, and water treatment plants. Infrastructure maintenance and improvement may be time- and money-consuming, and it may call for major government expenditure.

- Costs of insurance: Both homeowners' and business owners' insurance premiums may be affected by flooding. Living and working in flood-prone locations may become more costly after a flood as a result of rising insurance costs.

Flooding in Fort Lauderdale may have a big negative effect on the environment. The following are a few environmental effects of floods in Fort Lauderdale:

- Degradation of water quality: Sewage, chemicals, and garbage from industrial and domestic sources are just a few of the pollutants and toxins that may significantly rise in water bodies as a result of flooding. Reduced water quality, impairment to aquatic life, and health hazards for both people and animals may result from this.

- Flooding may result in erosion and sedimentation, which can cause topsoil loss, silt accumulation in streams, and infrastructure damage. Changes in water flow patterns may result from this as well, which may affect aquatic habitats and ecosystems.

- Habitat destruction: Natural habitats, such as wetlands and forests, which are crucial for biodiversity and ecosystem services, may suffer severe damage from flooding. Flooding may also result in fish and other aquatic creatures losing their home, which can have a ripple impact on the food chain.

- Climate change: In Fort Lauderdale, the effects of climate change, such as sea level rise, storm surges, and severe weather events, may be made worse by flooding. Further environmental deterioration and damage to human health and welfare may result from these effects.
- Beach erosion: Beach erosion is a result of flooding, which may destroy local ecosystems and harm the tourist sector. Beach erosion may result in the loss of sea turtle nesting habitat and beach habitat, as well as fewer recreational options for locals and tourists.

Flooding may have some effects on the Fort Lauderdale neighborhood. A few of the results are:

- Property Damage: Property damage is one of the most serious consequences of floods. Homes, companies, and other buildings may sustain significant damage by floodwaters, necessitating expensive repairs or perhaps making the property unusable.

- Economic Effects: Flooding may have a serious negative effect on the local economy. Companies could have to temporarily shut down, which would result in lost earnings. Also, the expenses of cleaning up after a flood may be high and may affect the local economy.

- Health and Safety Risks: Sewage, chemicals, and debris are just a few of the toxins that may pollute floodwaters. The population may be exposed to waterborne illnesses, infections, and other health dangers as a result of this pollution. Also, it can be dangerous for emergency personnel to reach individuals who need them because of how difficult the flooding makes it.

Displacement and Disruption: Flooding may significantly disrupt local communities and result in major relocation. As repairs are being done, residents could have to leave their houses or temporarily relocate. Stress, anxiety, and other mental health issues may result from this interruption.

CHAPTER 4

Solutions to Flooding in Fort Lauderdale and Strategies for preventing and managing flooding in Fort Lauderdale

Due to excessive rainfall, high tides, and storm surges, Fort Lauderdale is vulnerable to flooding, much like many other coastal communities. To safeguard the neighborhood and minimize any possible harm, flooding must be prevented and managed. The following are some methods for controlling and avoiding floods in Fort Lauderdale:

- Enhancing Drainage Systems: Upgrading drainage systems is one of the best strategies to control and avoid floods. This may be done in several ways, including by building more storm drains, cleaning up silt and debris from existing drainage channels, and expanding the functionality of current systems. Increased drainage system capacity and effectiveness may assist to lessen the effects of heavy rain and the possibility of floods.

- Putting Flood-Resistant Building Principles into Practice: Another efficient method for avoiding and controlling floods in Fort Lauderdale is to use flood-resistant construction principles. This might include utilizing materials that are resistant to flooding, providing waterproofing, and building on higher foundations. These steps may lessen the damage that flooding does to buildings and cut down on the expense of cleaning up and rebuilding after a storm.

- Creating Emergency Response Plans: To properly manage floods, emergency response plans must be created. This includes locating flood-prone regions, planning an escape route, and assembling emergency supplies. Plans for emergency response should also include communication methods to alert the public and guarantee the dispatch of emergency services when required.

- Green Infrastructure: Using green infrastructure techniques like installing green roofs, rain gardens, and bioswales may assist to lessen flooding's effects and the amount of runoff from storms. Flooding may be prevented by using green infrastructure to absorb water and decrease runoff into drainage systems.

- Development Control: Controlling development in flood-prone regions may assist to control and avoid floods. This may be accomplished via zoning regulations and construction standards that limit growth in flood-prone regions. Enforcing laws governing the development of structures and other infrastructure in these regions may also aid in ensuring that they are flood-resistant and able to withstand the effects of floods.

Infrastructure and engineering flood control measures

Due to its low height and closeness to the shore, Fort Lauderdale, which is situated in South Florida, is susceptible to floods. Many infrastructural and technical solutions might be deployed for flood control in Fort Lauderdale to handle this problem.

- Sea Walls: Building sea walls is a practical approach to stop flooding in low-lying places. These barriers between the ocean and land are designed to resist the power of waves and tides.
- Stormwater Management Systems: The use of stormwater management systems may aid in regulating water flow during times of intense rainfall. To collect extra water, this may include building retention ponds and installing drainage systems.
- Raised Roads and Walkways: In locations that are prone to flooding, elevated roads and walkways may be constructed to minimize floods. Water may be allowed to flow below these structures, preventing water from building up on the surface.

- Green Infrastructure: The use of green infrastructure may assist Fort Lauderdale's flooding problems to be lessened. This might include using rain gardens, permeable pavement, and green roofs to soak up extra water.

- Flood Barriers: In locations with a high danger of flooding, flood barriers might be erected. To stop water from entering uhouses and buildings, these barriers may be put in place during times of severe rain.

- Coastal Restoration: By acting as a natural defense against storm surges and sea level rise, the restoration of coastal ecosystems may assist to lessen the consequences of floods. This may include restoring coral reefs, salt marshes, and mangrove forests.

- Public Education and Awareness: Increasing public knowledge and awareness is a good strategy to stop floods in Fort Lauderdale. People may be informed about the potential of flooding and given instructions on how to be ready for and handle flooding emergencies.

Ultimately, the consequences of flooding in Fort Lauderdale may be lessened through a mix of engineering and infrastructural improvements, as well as more public knowledge and education.

Best practices for managing land use and urban development

Critical to a city's sustainable growth is an urban planning and land use management. The following best practices for efficient urban planning and land use management may be used in Fort Lauderdale:

- Implementing comprehensive planning may assist to make sure that the city's expansion and development are in line with its long-term goals. This may include creating a master plan that outlines the aims and objectives of the city and directs land-use choices.

- Smart Growth: Compact, walkable, and mixed-use development may be encouraged by putting smart growth ideas into practice. This may lessen the need for driving a vehicle, cut carbon emissions, and encourage healthier living.

- Transit-Oriented Development (TOD): TOD may be used to encourage sustainable modes of transportation including walking, bicycling, and public transportation. This may include the construction of dense, mixed-use buildings close to transportation hubs.
- Green infrastructure: By putting it in place, we can lessen the consequences of climate change and encourage sustainable growth. To lessen stormwater runoff and improve air quality, this might include integrating green roofs, rain gardens, and permeable pavement.
- Community Involvement: Including the community in land use choices may help to ensure that they are in line with their requirements and preferences. To promote public involvement in the planning process, this may include creating community outreach initiatives, public gatherings, and seminars.

- Preservation of Historic Sites: The preservation of historic sites may support sustainable development while preserving the city's cultural legacy. This may include locating and safeguarding historical sites, including structures and natural settings, as well as using tactics for adaptive reuse.
- Zoning and development regulations may be put into place to control land use and development in a way that supports sustainability. This may include the introduction of zoning districts, such as mixed-use and transit-oriented areas, that promote sustainable development.

In conclusion, Fort Lauderdale can support sustainable urban planning and land use management by implementing comprehensive planning, smart growth, transit-oriented development, green infrastructure, community participation, protection of historic sites, and zoning and development rules. These best practices may contribute to the development of a resilient, livable, and sustainable city for both the present and the future.

CHAPTER 5

The necessity of ongoing research and innovation in flood protection and management is emphasized in this call to action for community members, policymakers, and stakeholders.

We all play a crucial part in determining how our societies will develop as community members, decision-makers, and stakeholders. We must cooperate and take action to bring about change, whether it is in the realm of social, economic, or environmental challenges. To change things, we may do the following crucial things:

Join neighborhood groups or participate in volunteer work to better the lives of persons in your neighborhood. Also, you may participate in local politics and town hall meetings, where you can voice your concerns and speak out.

Consider the positions of political candidates on critical topics and support policies that reflect your views. Vote for candidates whose priorities include the welfare of their supporters and the advancement of values-based legislation.

Promote change by speaking out about topics that are important to you and by supporting advocacy campaigns that seek to transform society for the better. You may send letters to your elected officials, sign petitions, and take part in demonstrations and rallies.

Minimize your environmental effect by lowering your carbon footprint and supporting laws that put sustainability first. This might include using the bus, cutting down on trash, and supporting renewable energy sources.

Educate both yourself and others: Keep up with current affairs and look for other points of view. Encourage critical thinking and open-mindedness by imparting your expertise to others. Together, we can take these steps to build a brighter future for our families, our communities, and future generations. Let's all take action and be accountable for the world we live in.

The significance of ongoing innovation in flood control and prevention.

Given that Fort Lauderdale, Florida is situated in a low-lying coastal region that is vulnerable to flooding during severe weather events like hurricanes and torrential downpours, flooding is nothing new to the city. To reduce the hazards connected with flooding, the city must maintain its research and innovation in flood prevention and management.

Keeping up with the fast-changing environment is one of the main reasons why it is crucial to conduct ongoing research and innovation in flood prevention and management. Flood prevention and control measures must be continuously updated to stay successful given the rising frequency and severity of weather events brought on by climate change.

Moreover, new, more effective flood control and prevention techniques may be found thanks to research and innovation. For instance, the city should investigate the use of green infrastructure, such as bioswales and rain gardens, which can absorb precipitation and lessen the likelihood of floods. Research and innovation may also assist increase the precision of flood prediction models. By increasing the precision of flood forecasts, the city may take preemptive steps to avoid or lessen flood damage, such as deploying sandbags or evacuating citizens.

The economic and social effects of flooding may also be lessened through continuing research and innovation in flood management and prevention. Water damage may cause serious financial losses and disturb inhabitants' lives. The city can reduce these effects and safeguard the welfare of its citizens by strengthening flood prevention and control techniques.In conclusion, the security and well-being of Fort Lauderdale inhabitants must maintain research and innovation in flood prevention and management. The city can better prepare for and react to flooding disasters if it stays ahead of climate change, develops fresh flood protection techniques, increases the accuracy of flood predictions, and lessens the economic and social effects of floods.

Summary of significant insights from the book
The book **"Flooded in Fort Lauderdale:**
***Comprehensively Understanding the Causes,
Impacts, and Solutions"*** provides information
on the reasons for the flooding in the city as well
as its effects and solutions. These are the main
ideas to remember from the book:

- Many causes contribute to flooding in Fort
  Lauderdale, including sea level rise, storm
  surges, prolonged periods of severe rain,
  and poor infrastructure.

- Significant effects of flooding in Fort
  Lauderdale include dangers to the public's
  health, property damage, business
  disruption, and resident eviction.

- The building of sea walls, the adoption of
  stormwater management systems, the
  restoration of coastal ecosystems, the
  placement of flood barriers, the
  encouragement of public awareness and
  education, and other measures are only a
  few that the city may take to solve the
  problem of flooding.

- The promotion of sustainable urban planning and land use management in Fort Lauderdale may be aided by comprehensive planning, smart growth, transit-oriented development, green infrastructure, community participation, protection of historic sites, and zoning and development rules.
- The effective implementation of measures to alleviate flooding in Fort Lauderdale depends on collaboration between the local government, community groups, companies, and citizens.

Ultimately, the book emphasizes how urgent it is to solve flooding in Fort Lauderdale and offers a road map for the community's sustainable and resilient future.